Animal Wisdom: Practical Guide to Living and Manifesting Instinct

Preface

In an increasingly complex society, where decisions are often guided by rational logic and quantifiable data, we often find ourselves drifting away from that inner voice that knows wisdom without the need for explanations. It is there that instinct resides, a primordial force that flows through us, an ancestral memory of intrinsic wisdom that connects every living being.

This book, "Animal Wisdom: Practical Guide to Living and Manifesting Instinct," is an invitation to explore the fascinating and often overlooked world of our deepest nature. Through the pages of this guide, we journey together through the evolutionary origin of instinct, challenge the chains of modern society that often repress it, and discover the science that supports its power.

Our goal is clear: to help the reader rediscover the strength of instinct and learn to listen to it with respect and awareness. Each chapter is a step on the path to a profound understanding of this internal connection, providing not only theoretical information but also practical advice for integrating instinct into daily life.

The book not only explores the individual aspect of instinct but goes further, examining how this primordial force can be a guiding thread in connecting with others and in the harmony of the entire universe. Through challenges, mistakes, and fear, we learn that instinct is a reliable companion, a guide that can transform obstacles into opportunities for growth and learning.

In the final chapter, we project our gaze into the future, exploring how we can keep this connection with instinct alive in the long term, adapting to life's changes and challenges. The journey with instinct is a continuous path, an invitation to live in harmony with our most authentic nature and to manifest the innate wisdom that resides in each of us.

We hope that this book is not only a source of knowledge and inspiration but also a practical guide for those ready to explore the depths of their animal wisdom. May every reader embark on their journey with instinct, discovering a world of possibilities, personal growth, and universal connection. Safe travels!

Chapter 1: The Origin of Instinct

In the Heart of Primeval Nature: Unveiling the Evolutionary Roots of Instinct

In an intricate dance of adaptations and survival, instinct has manifested as an evolutionary masterpiece, weaving the invisible thread that connects living beings to a distant past. In this chapter, we delve into the depths of primeval nature, exploring the origins of instinct and its crucial role in the survival of organisms.

The Dance of Cells: Primordial Purpose in the Evolution of Life

For millennia, instinct has played a crucial role as a guide in vital decisions, shaping the very course of evolution. By analyzing the intricacies of cells, the true architects of this extraordinary phenomenon, we can understand how instinct has acted as a compass in the relentless pursuit of survival.

Through the microscope of evolutionary biology, we enter the secrets of the early forms of instinct. We examine how these innate responses emerged and adapted to face the ever-changing challenges of the environment. Instinct, as a primordial force, has influenced natural selection, shaping species and contributing to the extraordinary diversity we observe today.

From primordial cells to the complex neural networks of more evolved living beings, instinct has been the common thread that has united life in a symphony of adaptation and survival. Examining these dynamics, we can appreciate the crucial role of instinct in ensuring the continuity of life through the ages.

Today, as we explore the past of instinct through the prism of evolutionary biology, we can also reflect on how this ancient companion still influences our daily decisions. Instinct, though often hidden beneath the veil of modernity, continues to guide us, influencing choices that can shape our destiny and the course of our society's evolution.

Through this analysis of the roots of instinct, we can gain a deeper perspective on the force that has shaped the natural world. Unveiling the mysteries of its origin, we can learn to respect its power and listen to its voice in our modern existence. Instinct, ancient and timeless, persists as a beacon in the depths of our biology, illuminating humanity's path through the labyrinth of life.

Species Union: Deep Connections between Human and Animal Instinct

Instinct, that ancestral whisper resonating in every fiber of our being, is not an exclusive privilege of humanity. Let's explore the surprising similarities between human instinct and that of other animals, highlighting how this primordial force connects us to a vast array of living creatures.

From the epic migrations of birds to the intricate hunting strategies of predators, we are immersed in a world where instinct is the common denominator that traverses the animal kingdom. In the organized flight of a flock of birds, we reveal impeccable synchronization, an aerial ballet orchestrated by the migratory instinct that guides these creatures across incredible distances. In the nocturnal hunt of a predator, we discover the millimetric precision of the predatory instinct, shaped by evolution to ensure success in survival.

Yet, as we explore these manifestations of instinct in our life companions on Earth, we find that the essence of human instinct resides in the same evolutionary roots. Instinct guides our decisions, informs our actions, and shapes our perception of the world. In essence, we are part of a broader symphony of creatures, united by an invisible thread of instinct that resonates through the fabric of life itself.

This journey invites us to look beyond superficial differences and recognize the deep connection we share with other inhabitants of this planet. Instinct, a universal language engraved in the DNA of every creature, connects us to a vast heritage of wisdom that transcends linguistic and cultural barriers.

Through this exploration of similarities between human and animal instinct, we come closer to a deeper understanding of our role in the delicate balance of nature. In this shared connection, we can find inspiration to honor and protect our planet, recognizing that instinct is a force that unites us in a universal harmony.

Deep Past: Instinct as a Link to the History of Being

In this journey into the depths of time, we unveil how instinct has become a precious link to our most distant past. We explore the traces of this ancient companion in the myths and legends of ancient cultures, revealing how humanity has always recognized instinct as a sacred gift and a guardian of ancestral wisdom.

Through the mists of time, tales emerge that celebrate instinct as a divine power, a reflection of the intrinsic connection between humans and the natural world. In the myths of ancient civilizations, we discover how instinct was personified in deities guiding heroes through epic trials, symbolizing courage, and serving as a beacon in moments of uncertainty.

In the legends of indigenous peoples who have inhabited distant lands, we find respect for instinct as a reliable guide in everyday life and crucial decisions. The ancients regarded instinct as a gift from the spirits, a force that could be honored and listened to for navigating life's challenges.

The call of instinct is woven into the fabric of epic tales, where heroes follow the beat of the wild heart, guided by innate intuition that leads them through labyrinths of adventures. Instinct becomes a guiding light in the dark nights of the unknown, a reliable compass that orients humanity through the ages.

As we explore these legends surrounding instinct, we recognize that, even in the modern era, this connection to the past persists. Instinct is more than a reflection of our past; it is a living force that continues to flow into our lives, a river that runs through the fabric of our existence.

Through these ancient stories, we come closer to a universal truth: instinct has been a constant companion through the epochs, a witness to overcome challenges, celebrate victories, and learn lessons. We look to this past with gratitude, acknowledging the legacy of instinct as a precious gift that connects us to the very roots of our humanity.

Innate Power: Instinct as a Guide in the Present and Future

We conclude this chapter by taking a look at the present and the future, recognizing instinct as a powerful innate tool that goes beyond mere physical survival. Through evolution, we have come to understand that instinct is a beacon guiding us in daily choices and the realization of our deepest desires.

In the fabric of our present, instinct manifests as a trusted advisor, influencing decisions that shape our path. In a rapidly evolving world, instinct becomes a reliable compass, helping us navigate the challenges of modernity and seize the opportunities that arise.

Looking to the future, we recognize that instinct is not only a force of the past but also a precious ally that accompanies us in building tomorrow. In realizing

our dreams and ambitions,
instinct emerges as a powerful
catalyst, urging us to explore
uncharted territories and
overcome our own limitations.

In this intricate balance between
past, present, and future, instinct
reveals itself as a gift that
connects us to a long and rich
history of life. It is an inheritance
passed down through the ages, a
deep bond that unites us with all
the creatures that have walked
before us. Every pulse of instinct
is an echo of ancient voices
inviting us to honor the innate
wisdom flowing in the veins of our
existence.

Therefore, as we embark on our
journey into the future, let us
embrace instinct as a faithful
companion. Let us listen to it with
respect and awareness, aware
that within it lies the power to
guide us toward a deeper
personal realization and connect
us to a shared destiny with all that

lives. Instinct, with its intrinsic beauty and unwavering guidance, continues to illuminate the path we tread, uniting past, present, and future in an eternal symphony of life.

Chapter 2: Modern Society and the Suppression of Instinct

Social Filters: Pressures and Conformity in the Modern Era

In the frenetic age of modern society, where technological progress clashes with the deepest roots of human nature, we explore how instinct is often stifled under the weight of social expectations. The pressures to conform to predefined standards and the fear of judgment often hinder the free and authentic expression of instinct.

In this era of constant digital connection, humanity finds itself facing a paradoxical disconnection from its primal impulses. The race for progress and conformity to social norms can lead to a distortion of instinct, reducing it to an indecipherable whisper in the chaos of modern life.

Social expectations, often based on predetermined concepts of success, can act as invisible chains that limit the freedom of instinct. The fear of social judgment can make it challenging to listen to that inner voice that guides towards authentic personal achievements.

Our attempt to adapt to a standardized lifestyle, to follow predetermined paths without considering instinct, can lead to an inner emptiness and a lack of connection with our true essence. Instinct, our ancient ally in the quest for survival, struggles against the barriers of modernity, seeking to emerge in a world that often prefers rationality to innate wisdom.

However, by recognizing this challenge, we can begin to reverse the trend. Learning to recognize and honor our instinct can open us up to a more authentic and fulfilling life. Freeing instinct from the chains of social conformity can lead to a renewed sense of freedom and awareness.

Through awareness of how modern society can stifle instinct, we can embark on a journey of rediscovering this vital force. Instinct, when listened to attentively, can become a precious guide in navigating the complex seas of modern life. In this rediscovery, we can hope to find the golden thread of our authenticity, woven into the rich and intricate fabric of life.

The Theater of Judgment: How the Fear of Judgment Affects Instinct

Through in-depth analysis, we expose the pervasive fear of social judgment, acting as a paralyzing force against spontaneous instinct. We examine how society has constructed a stage where every move is scrutinized, leading many to suppress their instinct for fear of exclusion or criticism.

Social judgment, like a double-edged sword, creeps into the folds of our psyche, fueling the fear of rejection and disapproval. In this context, instinct, which should be a free guiding force, is often trapped in the cage of others' expectations.

Modern society, with its predefined standards of success and happiness, creates a fertile ground for the fear of judgment. Social media, in particular, serves as virtual showcases where everyone is called upon to present a curated and filtered version of themselves. This digital environment amplifies the pressure to conform, pushing many people to sideline their authentic instinct in favor of an acceptable representation.

The fear of being excluded, of being judged as different or not meeting social standards, can become a powerful brake against the free expression of instinct. People may find themselves sacrificing their authenticity on the altar of social acceptance, ignoring the instinct that, on the contrary, could lead to a more authentic and fulfilling life.

Exploring this dynamic, we invite deep reflection on the roots of the fear of social judgment. Perhaps, in confronting this fear, we can begin to free instinct from the chains of external approval. By embracing our uniqueness and allowing instinct to emerge without fear, we may discover new dimensions of personal fulfillment and human connection.

In this journey to liberate ourselves from the oppression of social judgment, let us seek to create a space where instinct can flourish without fear. Only then can we truly savor the sweet melody of our authenticity, without being drowned in the noise of external judgment.

The Conformity Paradox: Suppression of Instinct and Associated Risks

We now delve into the psychological consequences of suppressing instinct, exposing the risks associated with this process. From developing symptoms of stress and anxiety to a pervasive sense of personal dissatisfaction, the chapter reveals the paradox of conformity and how modern society, despite its orientation towards progress, can often undermine individual well-being.

The suppression of instinct can act as a subtle poison, infiltrating the soul and manifesting in a range of deleterious psychological consequences.

Stress, a result of the constant struggle against natural instinct, develops as a reaction to the internal conflict between what we feel we want and what society tells us to do. This chronic stress can have damaging effects on mental health, increasing the risk of conditions such as anxiety and depression.

Anxiety, often a silent companion of suppressed instinct, can emerge as a response to internal discord. The fear of not being accepted or failing to meet social expectations can generate a constant state of apprehension, undermining mental tranquility and hindering the ability to fully enjoy daily experiences.

The sense of personal dissatisfaction is another tangible consequence of suppressing instinct. When we strive to conform to standards that go against our nature, the result is often an inner void, a feeling that something is wrong despite external successes. The search for meaning and authenticity can become a daunting challenge when instinct is constantly relegated to the background.

The conformity paradox becomes evident when we realize that, although modern society is oriented towards progress and innovation, its model of success often relies on uniform and stereotyped standards. The consequence is that, as we advance as a society, we may simultaneously regress in our individual well-being.

Through this critical examination, we seek to stimulate deep reflection on the need to balance social progress with consideration for individual psychological well-being. The liberation of instinct can be seen as a form of resistance against forces that would homogenize human individuality. Only by embracing our authenticity can we hope to overcome the psychological barriers imposed by the suppression of instinct and embark on a path towards a more satisfying and meaningful life.

The Road to Conformity: The Danger of Predetermined Norms

Through examples from everyday life, we explore how predetermined social norms create a prepackaged path that, in many cases, hinders the free flow of instinct. Examining the danger of following in the footsteps of others without questioning our instinct, we risk losing the richness and diversity of individual experiences.

Imagine a common situation: the choice of a career. Often, society promotes a traditional view of success tied to specific professions. Many follow this predefined track, unaware that instinct might push them towards alternative, perhaps less conventional but more in tune with their true passions and abilities.

In the realm of relationships, social norms can dictate how romantic encounters should unfold and what the standards of success are. Blindly following these conventions can cause us to miss the opportunity to authentically connect with people and to listen to our true emotional inclinations.

In the creative realm, social expectations can limit expressive freedom. The fear of judgment can push artists, writers, or musicians to conform to predetermined standards rather than follow their creative instinct. In doing so, we risk losing the beauty of artistic and cultural diversity that comes from the free expression of instinct.

In the context of daily decisions, such as choosing clothing or hobbies, we are often conditioned by dominant social norms. Personal instinct, which might suggest more authentic and meaningful choices, can be stifled by uncritical adherence to predefined patterns.

These examples highlight the intrinsic risk of passively following social norms without listening to our instinct. The result can be a society of individuals following uniform paths, losing the richness of human diversity and unique experiences.

Reflecting on these scenarios, we encourage greater awareness of social influences and a renewed commitment to listening to individual instinct. Only by embracing our uniqueness can we hope to broaden the landscape of possibilities, contributing to a more inclusive, vibrant, and authentic society.

The Camouflage of Instinct: How Suppression Hides Behind Facades

We now reveal the skillful masks behind which suppressed instinct hides. We examine how modern society often encourages the construction of facades that conceal the true nature of the individual, leading to a loss of connection with one's authentic self.

In the race toward social conformity, many individuals find themselves wearing elaborate masks chosen to fit predefined standards. These masks can take various forms: the mask of success, hiding inner challenges behind an appearance of perfection; the mask of happiness, masking personal difficulties behind a radiant smile; or the mask of normality, seeking to blend in with social expectations, even at the cost of sacrificing authenticity.

The pressures of modern society often push people to build these intricate facades. The fear of social judgment, combined with the desire for belonging and acceptance, can lead to the adoption of behaviors and roles that are far from internal truth. In this process, authentic instinct is stifled under the weight of external expectations, leaving behind a filtered and distorted version of the self.

The masks, while they may provide temporary comfort or social adaptation, ultimately create a fracture between the individual and their authentic essence. The loss of connection with one's inner self can lead to a sense of emptiness and dissatisfaction, as the person continues to seek appreciation and recognition externally,

ignoring the richness of their internal instinct.

This phenomenon not only impacts the individual but also contributes to the formation of a society where interactions often occur between masks, rather than authentic beings.

The lack of transparency and distrust toward human vulnerability can weaken relational bonds, fueling a culture of appearance rather than substance. Exploring these masks is an invitation to deep reflection on the nature of instinct and the need to rediscover the courage to be true. Only by abandoning the masks and embracing authenticity can we hope to reconnect with our deepest instinct and build meaningful relationships based on genuineness and mutual understanding.

A Conscious Approach: Freeing Instinct from the Social Cage

We conclude the chapter by offering a conscious approach to liberating instinct from the social cage. We provide practical strategies to overcome the fear of judgment, challenge predefined norms, and embrace a more authentic way of living, where instinct becomes a guiding force in the pursuit of happiness and personal fulfillment. Through an enlightening journey into contemporary society, this chapter aims to raise awareness of the influences undermining the free expression of instinct and to provide tools to unleash this primal force, allowing for a more authentic and fulfilling life.

Freeing Instinct: A Conscious Approach

- Society Awareness: The first step towards liberating instinct is awareness.

Recognizing the influences of society and predefined norms that limit authentic expression is the foundation for meaningful change.

- Inner Exploration: Dedicate time to inner exploration. Ask deep questions about what you truly desire, what your values are, and what authentically makes you happy. This process helps identify and connect with your instinct.

- Acceptance of Vulnerability: Freeing instinct requires courage and acceptance of one's vulnerability. Being authentic means being willing to show oneself to the world with all facets, without fearing others' judgment.

- Challenging Norms: Embrace the challenge of breaking free from the chains of predefined norms. Experiment with different ways of living, make decisions based on your instinct rather than external expectations. The challenge creates opportunities for growth and discovery.

- Building Authentic Communities: Seek connections with those who appreciate your authenticity. Building authentic communities creates a safe space where instinct can flourish without fear.

- Practicing Gratitude: Recognizing and appreciating your instinct is crucial. Practicing gratitude for experiences guided by instinct strengthens the bond with this primal force.

- On the Quest for an Authentic Life

In a world where social pressures often push us to conform, freeing instinct becomes a revolutionary act of authenticity. This journey toward personal fulfillment through listening to and expressing instinct is an invitation to a deeper and more satisfying life. Through awareness and intentional action, we can cultivate a society where everyone can live with the courage to follow their instinct, contributing to a world richer in diversity, understanding, and authenticity.

Chapter 3: The Science Behind Instinct

The Cerebral Orchestra: A Journey into Instinct Processing

We delve into the fascinating world of science to unveil the mysteries of instinct. We explore how the brain, with its intricate symphony of neurons and chemical signals, processes instinctive information, revealing the subtle mechanisms of this primal force.

The brain, the true stage of instinct, hosts an extraordinary performance guided by the symphony of neurons. In this intricate biological theater, we explore how the brain translates instinctive signals into tangible actions. The nervous system, woven into the fabric of this instinctive symphony, coordinates immediate responses that often precede rational awareness.

Key regions involved in instinct emerge as leading actors. The amygdala, the guardian of emotions, and the limbic system, responsible for behavioral responses, collaborate in an intricate ballet that influences how we perceive and respond to the world. The prefrontal cortex, the brain's decision center, plays a fundamental role in the instinctive process, processing information from emotional regions and transforming instinctive signals into conscious decisions or immediate actions.

The brain's language unfolds through the world of synapses and neurotransmitters. Brain chemistry, with substances like dopamine and serotonin, modulates the intensity and direction of instinctive responses, creating a unique biochemical choreography. We conclude the chapter by highlighting how instinct is a dynamic and continuous process, an evolving symphony shaped by experiences and adapted to the challenges of everyday life.

The Decision Center: Instinct and the Brain

We immerse ourselves in the analysis of the brain regions involved in instinct processing, highlighting the crucial role of the brain in translating instinctive signals into tangible actions. We explore how the amygdala, the limbic system, and other brain areas interact to form an intricate network guiding instinct-based decision-making.

The Cerebral Stage of Instinct

The brain is the stage where the drama of instinct unfolds. Brain regions become the protagonists of this performance, with the amygdala and the limbic system, in particular, leading the intricate dance of instinctive responses.

The Amygdala: Guardian of Emotions

Situated in the limbic system, the amygdala emerges as the guardian of emotions. Its role in identifying signals of danger and opportunity triggers instinctive responses that shape our behavior.

The Limbic System: Emotions and Behavior

The limbic system, involved in emotions and behavioral responses, interacts with the amygdala. This collaboration forms an intricate network that influences how we interpret the world and act based on instinctive impulses.

Other Involved Brain Regions

In addition to the amygdala and the limbic system, we explore other key brain regions involved in instinct processing. How do these regions integrate into the choreography of instinctive decisions? We discover how the brain works synergistically to translate instinctive impulses into tangible behaviors.

The Dance of Instinctive Decisions

Observing the dynamics of the dance of instinctive decisions. How does the brain orchestrate this symphony of instinctive responses, providing an illuminating perspective on the complexity of this neurobiological process?

Through this analysis of the brain regions involved in instinct, we delve into the subtle and fascinating mechanisms that define our ability to instinctively respond to the surrounding world.

Neurotransmitters and the Chemistry of Instinct: The Brain's Language

We delve into the chemical language of the brain, exploring the role of neurotransmitters in instinct. From dopamine to oxytocin, we reveal how these chemicals influence how we perceive and respond to external stimuli, shaping our instinct and emotional response.

The Chemical Language of the Brain

The brain communicates through an intricate chemical language, where neurotransmitters play a key role. These chemicals act as messengers between neurons, transmitting signals and facilitating communication within the nervous system.

Dopamine: The Substance of Pleasure and Motivation

Dopamine is often associated with pleasure and motivation. We explore how this chemical influences feelings of satisfaction and joy, creating connections between gratifying instinctive behaviors and the sense of well-being.

Serotonin: Regulator of Mood and Emotions

Serotonin plays a key role in regulating mood and emotions. We analyze how this chemical contributes to emotional stability, influencing our ability to instinctively respond to stressful or rewarding situations.

Noradrenaline: The Substance of Excitement and Alertness

Noradrenaline is involved in activating the body in alert situations. We see how this chemical influences our readiness and ability to instinctively respond to environmental stimuli, preparing us for danger.

Oxytocin: The Social and Affection Bond

Oxytocin is known for its role in promoting social and affectionate bonds. We examine how this chemical modulates our ability to instinctively connect with others, fostering meaningful relationships.

Endorphins: Well-being and Relaxation

Endorphins are involved in pain management and promoting well-being. We explore how these chemicals can modulate our instinctive response to stressful situations, promoting a state of relaxation and tranquility.

A Chemical Ballet in Instinct

We conclude by examining how these neurotransmitters dance together in the instinctive process. How do they combine to create a unique melody that guides our instinctive responses and actions?
Through this exploration of the brain's chemical language, we shed light on the biochemical influences shaping our instinct, emphasizing the complexity and beauty of this neurobiological symphony.

Nervous Connection: Intertwining Instinct and the Nervous System

In this section, we trace together the chain of command to the nervous system, examining how electrical signals and nerve impulses propagate to every cell, connecting instinct to your body. We explore the crucial role of sensory perception and motor response in expressing your instinct, demonstrating how this connection is essential for your instinctive response to the surrounding environment.

Your Nervous Chain of Command

Imagine your nervous system as a sophisticated chain of command, transmitting electrical signals and nerve impulses from one part of your body to another. We will explore how this intricate network is the vehicle through which your instinct manifests.

From Your Brain to Your Body: The Journey of Nerve Impulses

We will follow the path of nerve impulses traveling from your brain, the decision center, to every cell in your body. Through the spinal cord and peripheral nerves, these impulses will carry instinctive instructions to every part of you, coordinating a synergistic and instantaneous response.

Your Senses: Input for Your Instinct

Reflect on the fundamental role of your senses as input for your instinct. Your sensory organs transform external stimuli into electrical signals, initiating the process of interpretation and instinctive response. How does your brain translate this information into instinctive instructions?

Your Response: Output of Your Instinct

We explore together your motor response as the output of your instinct. How do nerve impulses activate your muscles and coordinate movements that reflect your instinctive response? Discover how your body, through motor response, expresses your instinct in the surrounding world.

Essential Connection: Your Instinct and Your Nervous System

We conclude by emphasizing the essential connection between your instinct and your nervous system. This dynamic relationship is vital for your ability to respond promptly, instinctively, and adaptively to the challenges and opportunities presented by the environment.

Through this exploration of your nervous chain of command, we seek to illuminate the synergy between your instinct and your nervous system, highlighting how this connection is fundamental to your instinctive expression and interaction with the world.

Neuroscience Studies: Illuminating the Crucial Importance of Instinct

Now we explore a fascinating world of scientific discoveries that have shed light on the crucial importance of instinct in your daily life. Neuroscience, with its pioneering research, offers us an extraordinary overview of how instinct plays a key role in shaping our thinking and behavior.

Illuminating Instinct Through Neuroscience

Imagine being in the laboratory of mind and brain scholars. Here, scientists have conducted illuminating experiments to understand how instinct manifests in every aspect of your life.

Complex Decisions and the Invisible Guidance of Instinct

In-depth studies have revealed that even in the most complex decisions, instinct plays an invisible yet powerful role. Your brain, with fascinating mastery, instinctively weighs options, guiding you towards choices that reflect the innate wisdom of your instinct.

Moments of Creativity: When Instinct Takes the Helm

Together, we explore those moments of creativity, those sparkling instances where inspiration seems to spring from nowhere. Neuroscience reveals that even behind the scenes, instinct is shaping your creative thinking, suggesting brilliant solutions and bold visions.

The Exploration of Studies and Discoveries

We navigate through studies that explore how instinct influences your way of perceiving the world and making decisions. From facial expressions to emotional reactions, from memory to decision-making, every aspect of your life is intertwined with instinct.

Instinct as a Reliable Guide

We conclude by reflecting on how neuroscience has clearly established that instinct is not just a companion on the journey but a reliable guide in your daily experience. Through an intricate neural ballet, your instinct reveals itself as a precious ally, fundamentally shaping your existence in ways that often escape conscious awareness.

In this fascinating journey through scientific research, we learn to recognize and appreciate the invaluable role that instinct plays in shaping your life. Are we ready to explore this intriguing world together?

Instinct and Creativity: The Brain's Alchemy of Genius

In this captivating chapter, we explore the extraordinary union of instinct and creativity, revealing how this dynamic duo is an endless source of inspiration and innovation. From observing brilliant minds to in-depth studies on creativity, we demonstrate how instinct is the fertile ground on which out-of-the-box thinking and solving complex problems thrive.

Instinct as a Creative Forge

Let's immerse ourselves in captivating stories of creative geniuses who, knowingly or unknowingly, have embraced the power of instinct in their revolutionary works. From visionary artists to enlightened scientific minds, instinct emerges as an irreplaceable ally in the quest for novelty and originality.

Studies on Creativity: The Subtle
Balance between Structure and
Chaos

Through in-depth studies on
creativity, we examine the delicate
balance between necessary
mental structure and the creative
freedom that instinct provides.
Discover how creative minds
navigate between order and
chaos, finding in instinct the key
to opening doors to new horizons
of thought.

**Scientific Approach:
Intertwining the Brain, Instinct,
and Creativity**

We conclude with an illuminating
scientific approach, offering the
reader an in-depth view of the
complexity of the brain and its
intertwined connection with
instinct. Through science, we gain
a deeper understanding of how
this primal force is intricately
linked to our biology,

fundamentally shaping how we live and perceive the world.

In this chapter, you will discover that instinct is not only the guardian of survival but also the secret mentor of creativity. Its subtle and powerful influence permeates the fabric of human thought, offering the key to unlocking the unlimited potential of your creative mind. Are we ready to explore this intriguing territory of the mind and instinct together?

Chapter 4: Listening to Instinct - The First Step

Instinct as an Inner Guide: An Invitation to Awareness

At the pulsating heart of this chapter, we immerse ourselves in the practice of listening to instinct, revealing its power as the crucial first step towards a more authentic and fulfilling life. With attentive eyes, we explore how instinct, often stifled by external voices and social expectations, can emerge as a potent inner guide if only we learn to listen.

The Silent Voice Within You

We begin by acknowledging that instinct speaks in a subtle language, a silent voice resonating within you. Through illuminating examples, we discover how this inner whisper can offer you wisdom and profound insights.

Nuances of Instinct: Distinguishing Noise from Reality

Together, we explore the nuances of instinct, learning to distinguish the noise of external influences from the pure reality of your instinct. Through practical exercises and guided reflections, I will lead you in the process of tuning into the authentic voice residing within you.

Breaking Mental Barriers: Unleashing Blocked Instinct

We tackle the mental barriers that often hinder instinctive listening. Together, we discover how to free blocked instinct, allowing this primal force to flow freely into your awareness.

Real-life Examples: Stories of Those Who Listened

I narrate real-life stories of individuals who embraced instinctive listening, recounting moments when they followed their sixth sense and the surprising results that ensued.

The Power of Saying Yes: Allowing Instinct to Lead

We conclude by highlighting the transformative power of saying yes to instinct, letting it guide your path. Through this act of trust, you'll discover how instinct can become a guiding beacon in your pursuit of an authentic and meaningful life.

In this chapter, I invite you on an intimate journey of self-exploration, a dance with your inner voice. Are we ready to lift the veil and discover together the revealing force of instinct?

Challenging Mental Barriers: Freeing Instinct from the Prison of the Mind

Together, we confront the mental barriers that sometimes prevent us from listening to instinct. We'll analyze fears, doubts, and cultural stereotypes that may cast doubt on the validity of our instinct. In this chapter, you'll discover practical strategies to overcome these obstacles, opening the door to a deeper connection with your instinctive self.

Exploring Fears that Block Instinct

We begin by addressing the fears that can serve as barriers to instinctive listening. We'll examine the roots of these fears, ranging from the fear of judgment to the fear of failure, revealing how understanding and confronting these emotions can pave the way for the liberation of instinct.

Doubts and Inner Challenges

We'll examine inner doubts that sometimes plague us when considering following our instinct. Through practical examples and case studies, we'll explore how to address these doubts and transform them into opportunities for greater self-understanding and awareness of our natural inclinations.

Cultural Stereotypes: Breaking the Chains

We'll also analyze cultural stereotypes that can negatively influence the perception of instinct. You'll learn how to recognize and challenge these stereotypes, opening the way to a freer and more authentic view of your instinctive self.

**Practical Strategies for
Unleashing Instinct**

We'll conclude by offering
practical strategies for
overcoming these mental barriers,
allowing instinct to emerge
clearly. Through mindfulness
exercises, guided meditations,
and holistic approaches, you'll be
guided in the process of freeing
blocked instinct.

Through this chapter, I invite you
to explore the inner terrain of your
fears and doubts, confronting the
obstacles that may separate you
from the innate wisdom of your
instinct. Are you ready to break
the chains and allow your instinct
to blossom freely?

**Breaking Social Chains: Freeing
Instinct from External Pressure**

Together, we explore how social
pressure can often limit the
freedom to follow instinct. In this
chapter, we'll analyze tangible

examples that show how breaking the chains of social conformity can allow instinct to emerge unrestricted. We'll also provide practical advice on facing the judgment of others and embracing authenticity.

The Invisible Chains of Conformity

We begin by unveiling the invisible chains of social conformity that can stifle instinct. We'll examine how others' expectations and predefined standards can create barriers to the free expression of your instinctive self.

Tangible Examples of Liberation

We'll narrate tangible stories of individuals who have broken the chains of social conformity, allowing instinct to flourish without restrictions. These examples will illuminate the path to individual freedom and inspire

the reader to consider similar
ways of liberating their instinct.

Facing Judgment with Confidence

We'll confront the challenge of others' judgment, offering practical advice on developing the confidence needed to face and overcome the fear of judgment. Through authenticity strategies, we'll guide you in the process of staying true to yourself despite external opinions.

The Embrace of Authenticity

We'll conclude by developing the theme of authenticity as a key to freeing instinct. Through practical exercises and guided reflections, we'll help you embrace your authenticity, opening the way to a more liberated and fulfilling expression of your instinct.

Through this chapter, I invite you to explore the courage to break the chains of social conformity, creating spaces for the emergence of your authentic instinct. Are you ready to free yourself from others' expectations and allow instinct to guide you to your true essence?

The Secret Language of Instinct: How to Identify Silent Signals

Together, we'll explore the secret language of instinct and learn to decipher its messages. Instinct often communicates with us through a whisper, a gentle voice trying to guide us. We'll examine real-life situations where instinct intervened, leading to wise and intuitive decisions that made the difference between success and failure, happiness and disappointment.

The Whisper of Instinct

First and foremost, we recognize that instinct communicates subtly. We'll narrate real-life stories that clearly illustrate the power of the language of instinct. These examples will serve as guiding lights, showing you how instinct can offer valuable insights in everyday decisions and more challenging situations.

Illuminating Examples

Through tangible examples, we'll highlight how instinct has guided individuals in crucial situations. These practical examples will demonstrate how active listening to instinct can lead to choices that reflect innate wisdom.

Training the Mind in Instinct

I'll provide practical exercises to train your mind to recognize and interpret instinctive signals. This consistent training process will make you increasingly adept at translating the secret language of instinct into concrete actions in your daily life.

The Art of Active Listening

We'll conclude by exploring the art of active listening to instinct. I'll guide you in creating a mental space conducive to connecting with your inner voice, allowing you to consciously welcome wisdom and insights.

Are we ready to immerse ourselves together in the secret language of instinct? Join this journey of self-exploration and discover how to decipher the messages your instinct has to offer.

Guided Exercises: Paths to Deeper Connections with Instinct

Guided exercises designed to help you tune into your instinct.

Each exercise is crafted to provide a concrete path for the development of a stronger instinctive awareness. Through practices such as instinctive meditation and guided reflection, we will overcome mental and social resistances together, opening the way to a more authentic connection with your instinct.

Exercise 1: Instinctive Meditation

I'll guide you through an instinctive meditation to help you focus on your inner voice. Through breath awareness and mental relaxation, you'll open your mind to a deeper listening to your instinct.

Exercise 2: Rediscovering Silence

We'll explore the importance of silence in connecting with instinct. Through guided reflection exercises, you'll learn to create mental spaces of silence that foster the emergence of instinctive intuitions.

Exercise 3: Dialogue with Instinct

I'll guide you in an exercise of dialogue with instinct, encouraging you to ask questions and listen to the answers that emerge from the depths of your consciousness. This exercise will strengthen your bond with the inner voice.

Exercise 4: Exploring Intuitive Places

We'll examine how exploring places that inspire intuition can amplify your instinctive awareness. I'll provide guidance on how to harness the energy of these places to strengthen your connection with instinct.

Exercise 5: Writing the Instinct Journal

I'll encourage you to keep an instinct journal, recording daily thoughts, feelings, and intuitions. This writing exercise will solidify the process of active listening and allow you to reflect on your experiences.

With these guided exercises, I invite you to explore and cultivate your connection with instinct. Take the time to embrace these moments of self-reflection and discovery.

Transformation Stories: Real-life Examples of Those Who Listened to Instinct

Through engaging life stories, we'll explore extraordinary transformations that have arisen from listening to instinct. Through courageous career decisions and relational choices, we'll delve into how proactive individuals have embraced their instinct, achieving surprising and often unexpected results.

Story 1: The Leap into the Unknown

Embark on your immersion with the story of Alessandra, a woman who decided to follow her instinct and leave a secure but unsatisfying career. Through the courage to explore the unknown, she discovered a passion that transformed her life and led to deeper professional and personal fulfillment.

Story 2: Rediscovered Love

Explore the story of Marco, an individual who listened to instinct in his relational journey. Through awareness of his intuitions, he rediscovered authentic love, breaking old patterns and opening up to a deeper and more meaningful connection.

Story 3: The Inner Journey

Follow the story of Elena, a soul traveler who listened to instinct in her inner journey. Through moments of reflection and meditation, she confronted deep fears and found inner peace that radically changed her perspective on life.

Story 4: Betting on Oneself

Meet Paolo, an entrepreneur who bet on himself by listening to instinct. Through calculated risks and decisions based on his inner voice, he transformed his business and achieved milestones that initially seemed impossible.

Story 5: Rebirth from Mistake

Conclude the chapter with the story of Marta, an individual who learned to consider mistakes as valuable lessons through instinct. Through resilience and active listening to the inner voice, she turned apparent failures into opportunities for personal growth.

These stories embody the transformative power of instinct. Each of them invites reflection on your own intuitions and considers how active listening to instinct can open unimaginable doors in our lives.

The Cycle of Listening: Continuing to Nurture the Connection with Instinct

We conclude this chapter with an invitation to continue the cycle of instinctive listening. We've explored fascinating life stories and shared practical exercises to help you connect with your inner voice. Now, we encourage you to make instinctive listening an integral part of your daily life.

Maintaining the Connection:

- Regular Practice: Dedicate regular time to listening exercises, such as instinctive meditation or keeping an instinct journal.

- Present-Moment Awareness: Cultivate awareness of the present moment, allowing instinct to emerge in daily decisions.

- Continuous Exploration: Be open to continuous exploration. New experiences provide new insights for active instinctive listening.

- Nurturing the Connection:

- Supportive Environment: Create an environment conducive to listening. Find quiet places and moments to reflect.

- **Support Circle:** Share your experiences with a support circle. Instinct can flourish in contexts of sharing and mutual support.
- **Continuous Learning:**

- **Lessons from Every Experience:** Consider every experience, both positive and negative, as an opportunity to learn from instinct.

- **Constant Adaptation:** Be flexible and adapt to changes. Instinct can guide you through new scenarios and challenges

Remember that instinctive listening is a continuous process of learning and personal growth. Through awareness and constant practice, you can increasingly unleash this primal force, opening new possibilities in the pursuit of a more authentic and meaningful life.

Chapter 5: The Role of Instinct in Personal Fulfillment

Instinct as a Guide to the Pinnacles of Personal Fulfillment

In this chapter, we lay the foundation for personal fulfillment through attentive and conscious listening to instinct. We explore how this powerful ally can be the driving force behind significant achievements and satisfying personal fulfillment.

The Journey to Fulfillment: Listening to Instinct as the First Step

We approach instinct as the key that unlocks the doors to personal fulfillment. We examine how deep listening to this inner companion can guide us towards unique and authentic paths, creating a bridge between who we truly are and who we want to become.

Instinct as a Personal Guide:

- Authenticity: Listening to instinct connects us with our deepest authenticity. When we allow ourselves to follow this internal guide, we reveal who we truly are to the world.

- Quest for Purpose: Instinct often directs us towards what truly impassions us, helping us discover our purpose and the direction of our lives.

Unique and Authentic Paths:

- Intuition-Guided Choices: Choices based on instinct often lead us outside conventional norms, paving the way for unique and personal paths.

- Exploration of New Horizons: Instinct invites us to explore new horizons, pushing us beyond the boundaries of our comfort zones to embrace the unknown.
- Creating a Bridge between the Present and the Future:

- Clear Vision: Active listening to instinct provides us with a clear vision of where we want to go, serving as a guide in our personal growth journey.

- Continuous Transformation: Following instinct implies accepting continuous transformation. Every step along the way represents another chapter in the story of our personal fulfillment.

- Through instinct, we discover an intrinsic key to unlocking our highest potential. It is a trusted companion that guides us through life's challenges and victories, transforming the journey of personal fulfillment into an authentic and meaningful experience.

Success Stories: When Instinct Becomes the Driving Force

Immerse yourself in engaging success stories, demonstrating how individuals enlightened by instinct have achieved extraordinary results. From entrepreneurial decisions to adventurous life choices, we explore how listening to instinct provided the necessary impetus to overcome challenges and realize otherwise unimaginable dreams.

**Entrepreneurial Decisions
Guided by Instinct:**

- Innovation and Creation: Successful entrepreneurs often attribute their boldest innovations and creations to deep listening to instinct, guiding them in unexpected directions.

- Calculated Risk-Taking: Instinct provides an element of calculated risk-taking, urging individuals to undertake challenges that, while seemingly risky, ultimately lead to extraordinary rewards.
- Overcoming Personal Challenges:

- Life Transformations: Stories of individuals who listened to their instinct at crucial moments, completely changing the direction of their lives and embracing significant transformations.

- Courageously Facing Challenges: Instinct becomes a beacon of courage in personal challenges, guiding individuals through tough times and leading them to a deeper realization of themselves.

Realization of Dreams:

- Unimaginable Dreams: Explore how instinct has allowed individuals to realize dreams that seemed unimaginable, transforming bold visions into tangible reality.

- Driving Force of Success: In many success stories, instinct emerges as the driving force that catalyzed crucial actions and decisions to achieve extraordinary milestones.

- Through these engaging stories, we hope to inspire you to listen to your instinct, considering it as a precious guide in your pursuit of success and personal fulfillment.

From Intuition to Action: Instinct as a Trigger for Meaningful Actions

We analyze how instinct is not merely a passive advisor but a catalyst that propels us into action. We explore how the connection with instinct can transform intuition into concrete actions, creating a direct link between the inner and outer worlds.

Instinct as a Catalyst for Action:

- Urge for Adventure: Instinct, when listened to attentively, becomes a force that propels towards bold adventures and new experiences, encouraging individuals to explore uncharted territories.

- Transforming Intuitions into Actions: We examine how instinct transforms inner intuitions and perceptions into concrete actions, allowing individuals to translate their deepest thoughts into tangible realities.
- Connection between Inner and Outer Worlds:

- Harmonizing Elements: Listening to instinct facilitates the harmonization between the inner world of emotions, aspirations, and intuitions and the outer world of opportunities and challenges.

- Guiding Exploration of the Outer World: Instinct becomes a compass guiding individuals in exploring the outer world, enabling them to make choices more aligned with their essence.

Fulfillment through Instinct-Guided Actions:

- Meaningful Actions: Explore how actions guided by instinct are often charged with meaning and coherence, contributing to personal fulfillment in profound ways.

- Authenticity in Behavior: Instinct, when translated into actions, creates an authentic manifestation of who one truly is, contributing to the building of sincere and gratifying relationships.

- Through this exploration, we hope to inspire you to consider instinct not only as an internal voice but as an engine that transforms thoughts and desires into meaningful and authentic actions.

Respecting Individuality: How Instinct Brings Forth Our Uniqueness

We examine how listening to instinct leads to the respect for our individuality. Through instinct-guided decisions, we discover how our peculiarities emerge and how personal fulfillment is closely connected with the acceptance and celebration of what makes us unique.

Instinct as a Guide to Self-Discovery:

- Rediscovery of Peculiarities: Attentive listening to instinct serves as a guide in rediscovering our unique peculiarities, highlighting the distinctive aspects of our personality.

- Self-Acceptance: Explore how following instinct fosters self-acceptance, encouraging individuals to embrace the characteristics that set them apart from others.

Connection between Instinct and Identity:

- Authenticity in Decisions: Instinct, when followed wholeheartedly, leads to authentic decisions that reflect who one truly is, allowing for a deeper connection with one's identity.

- Celebration of Diversity: Through stories of those who have embraced their instinct, we explore how

this celebration of individual diversity leads to greater satisfaction and personal fulfillment.
- The Reality of Our Uniqueness:

- Respect for Life Choices: Listening to instinct urges life choices that respect our individuality, contributing to the creation of a unique path of growth and development.

- Impact on Emotional Well-Being: Examine how consistency between instinct-guided decisions and our true nature contributes to emotional well-being, creating a solid foundation for personal fulfillment.

Celebrating Our Authenticity:

- Authenticity as the Key to Happiness: Through

examples of individuals who have embraced their authenticity, we highlight how this is a fundamental step toward a happier and more fulfilling life.

- Unique Contribution to the Universe: Conclude by reflecting on how respecting and following our instinct not only brings us closer to personal fulfillment but also contributes to a richer and more diversified mosaic in the universe.

- Through this exploration, we invite you to honor and respect your individuality, discovering how instinct can be the guiding light toward a deeper understanding of yourself.

The Balance Between Risk and Security: The Subtle Dance of Instinct

We explore the delicate balance between risk and security, addressing the fact that instinct often guides us into unknown territories. Through stories of individuals who embraced uncertainty, we demonstrate how instinct can be an ally even in seemingly risky situations, opening the door to unexpected opportunities.

Navigating the Unknown:

- Instinct as a Compass in the Unknown: We analyze how instinct is the reliable compass that guides us through uncertainty, allowing us to navigate confidently in uncharted territories.

- Stories of Courage and Risk: Through engaging

stories of individuals who followed their instinct even when the path seemed uncertain, we illustrate how courage in risk can lead to extraordinary life experiences.

Opportunities in Moments of Risk:

- Risk as a Door to Opportunities: We examine how instinct, courageously followed, can reveal hidden opportunities behind the doors of risk, showing that what appears dangerous can be a path to personal growth.

- Courage to Embrace Imperfection: Reflect on how listening to instinct encourages us to embrace imperfection and open up to life's imperfections, transforming risky situations into moments of growth.

Lesson from Uncertainty:

- Unpredictable Outcomes: Illustrate how instinct, even if it may lead to unexpected results, is a valuable companion in the pursuit of our true calling and happiness.

- Security in Embracing the Unsolvable: Conclude by reflecting on how true security lies in the ability to embrace the unsolvable, recognizing that the path of instinct can lead to a wealth of experiences and realizations.

- Through this exploration, we invite you to consider the fundamental role of risk in listening to instinct, discovering that, at times, it is in uncertainty that the most meaningful opportunities are found.

Personal Fulfillment as a Continuous Process: Nurturing the Connection with Instinct Over Time

We conclude this chapter by emphasizing that personal fulfillment is a continuous and dynamic process. We offer concrete strategies to nurture the connection with instinct over time, recognizing that our aspirations and desires can evolve. Instinct, as an inner compass, guides us through the different phases of life.

Nurturing the Connection Over Time:

- Adaptability and Personal Growth: Explore how adaptability is a key virtue in maintaining a deep connection with instinct. The process of adaptation allows us to grow alongside our evolving instinct.

- Respect for Life Phases: Reflect on respect for the various phases of life and how instinct can provide valuable guidance on which path to take in each of them.

A Continuous Journey:

- The Cycle of Listening: Illustrate how listening to instinct is not a single act but rather a continuous cycle. Each phase of life presents new challenges and opportunities, and instinct is the trusted companion guiding us through these cycles.

- Strategies to Maintain the Connection: Offer practices and strategies to maintain the connection with instinct in daily life, encouraging the reader to make instinctive listening an integral part of their lifestyle.

- Instinct's Guidance to Personal Fulfillment:

- Reflection on Personal Progression: Conclude by reflecting on personal progression and how constant listening to instinct is the key to reaching ever higher peaks in our pursuit of personal fulfillment.

- The Journey Towards an Authentic and Fulfilling Life: Invite the reader to embark on a continuous journey toward an authentic and fulfilling life, where instinct reveals itself as the primary engine for achieving deeper personal fulfillment.

Through reading this chapter, we hope you are inspired by the awareness of the essential role of instinct in your quest for meaningful personal fulfillment. Success stories emerge clearly, emphasizing that listening to instinct is the fundamental step towards reaching the highest peaks of personal fulfillment.

Chapter 6: Confronting Fear and Failure

The Inevitable Apprehension: Exploring Fear as the Unyielding Companion of Instinct

In this chapter, we delve into the intricate territory of fear, acknowledging how it often serves as an unwavering companion along the path of instinct. We analyze the deep roots of fear, exploring its impact on our ability to listen to and follow instinct.

The Internal Foe: How Fear Hinders Instinctual Listening

We will examine how fear becomes an internal adversary, limiting our capacity to listen to instinct. Through concrete examples, we will highlight how the fear of failure can act as a distorting filter, obscuring the clarity of instinct and leading us to decisions based on irrational anxieties.

The Fear of Failure as a Hurdle:

- Analysis of Fear: We will delve into the roots of the fear of failure and how this emotion can embed itself deeply in our subconscious. We will explore how modern society may contribute to intensifying this fear.

- The Filter of Fear: We will describe how the fear of failure can act as a filter through which we perceive and evaluate our options. This filter can alter our perception of instinct, causing us to ignore crucial signals.

Irrational Anxieties and Distortions:

- Lesson from Irrational Anxieties: We will examine irrational anxieties that arise from the fear of failure, analyzing how these anxieties can distort our evaluation of situations and influence decisions.

- Impact on Decision-Making Process: We will illustrate how fear can influence the decision-making process, leading us to avoid potentially rewarding opportunities or pursue paths that go against our deepest instincts.

Confronting Fear:

- Strategies to Manage Fear: We will offer practical strategies for managing the fear of failure, including mindfulness exercises and coping techniques. These strategies aim to free instinct from the grip of fear, allowing for purer and more authentic listening.

- Transforming Fear into Strength: We will explore how we can transform the fear of failure into a motivating force rather than a paralyzing one. Instead of viewing it as an obstacle, we will learn to use fear as a catalyst for change and growth.

- We conclude the chapter by encouraging you to explore your relationship with the fear of failure and develop the necessary skills to face it with courage. Liberating instinct from this fear is a fundamental step to allow it to flow freely and guide you towards personal fulfillment.

Rewriting the Narrative: Redesigning the Meaning of Failure

We examine how we can rewrite the narrative of failure, stripping it of negative connotations. Through examples of successful figures who have experienced setbacks, we show how failure can be seen as a crucial step on the path to success, rather than a definitive verdict.

The Power of Comeback: How Failure Nurtures the Resilience of Instinct

We analyze how failure can nurture the resilience of instinct. By understanding failures as valuable lessons, we highlight how instinctual listening becomes more robust and insightful, fueled by the lessons learned through overcome challenges.

The Courage to Persist:
Confronting Fear as an Integral
Part of the Journey with Instinct

We conclude the chapter by
emphasizing the courage required
to continue following instinct
despite persistent fear. We
provide a framework for
understanding that fear is an
inevitable travel companion but
with the right perspective and
skills acquired through failure, we
can still move forward confidently
along our path of listening and
realizing instinct.

By openly confronting fear and
failure, this chapter offers not only
practical strategies but also a
transformative perspective on the
relationship between these
challenges and instinctual
listening. Recognizing fear as an
integral part of the journey with
instinct becomes a key to
overcoming obstacles and fully
embracing the richness of this
inner connection.

Chapter 7: Learning from Instinct - Lessons from Past Mistakes

The Alchemy of Errors: How Mistakes Transform into Life Masters

In this chapter, let's immerse ourselves in the alchemy of errors, recognizing that every misstep can become a precious life master. We will explore how instinct, even when it seems to lead us down the wrong paths, can actually offer fundamental lessons for personal and spiritual growth.

The Perspective of Reflection: Revisiting Errors with Fresh Eyes

We examine how the perspective of reflection, looking back on past errors, allows us to revisit them with fresh eyes. Through case studies, we will analyze how individuals enlightened by instinct have faced their own mistakes with an open mind, transforming them from obstacles into steps on the ladder of personal growth.

Beyond Guilt: Overcoming the Sense of Guilt Associated with Errors

We address the theme of guilt associated with errors. We explore how instinct can help us overcome guilt by understanding that every mistake is an opportunity for learning. We provide strategies to embrace errors without condemning ourselves but rather learning from them with wisdom.

Success Case Studies: Errors as Bridges to Success

Through case studies, we demonstrate how successful individuals have used errors as bridges to success. We will explore how instinct has guided them through challenging situations, turning obstacles into springboards for new opportunities and achievements.

Hidden Lessons: How Instinct Reveals Profound Truths through Errors

We examine how instinct can reveal profound truths through errors. Through reflections on past choices, we show how instinct can serve as an inner guide, leading us to revelations that, although painful, are essential for our spiritual and emotional growth.

Rebirth from Error: How Instinct Fosters Personal Regeneration

We explore the concept of rebirth from error, highlighting how instinct fosters personal regeneration. We analyze stories of individuals who, through the process of learning from mistakes, have experienced profound growth, transforming into more conscious and authentic versions of themselves.

Embracing Vulnerability: How Instinct Teaches Us to Welcome Imperfection

We conclude the chapter by reflecting on the embrace of vulnerability, a fundamental aspect of learning from instinct. We explore how instinct teaches us to welcome imperfection and embrace our humanity, making every mistake an essential piece in the mosaic of our existence.

Through this chapter, readers will be guided to reconsider the perception of errors as failures, learning to see them as bridges to deeper personal growth and gaining a sharper understanding of instinct as a wise guide through life's intricate paths.

Chapter 8: Respect for Instinct and the Universal Community

The Universal Bond: How Instinct Connects Us to the Entire Universe

In this chapter, we explore the powerful bond between instinct and the entire universe. We will analyze how respectful listening to instinct not only contributes to our personal fulfillment but also extends to connecting with other beings and maintaining balance in the universe as a whole.

Instinct as an Empathic Bridge: Connecting with Other Beings

We examine how instinct can act as an empathic bridge, allowing us to connect more deeply with other beings. Through examples of instinctive empathy, we demonstrate how respectful listening to instinct can be the foundation for more authentic and understanding relationships.

The Gift of Presence: How Instinct Fosters Social Awareness

We delve into the concept of the gift of presence, highlighting how instinct fosters social awareness. By attentively listening to instinct, we can become agents of positive change in our communities, building meaningful bonds based on understanding and collaboration.

The Responsibility of Instinct: Contributing to Collective Well-being

We explore the responsibility associated with instinct, emphasizing how its correct interpretation and application can contribute to collective well-being. We analyze how decisions made by listening to instinct can positively influence society, promoting values of solidarity, equity, and sustainability.

Universal Harmony: Balance through Respectful Instinct

We discuss the role of instinct in maintaining universal harmony. Exploring how respect for instinct, both at an individual and collective level, can contribute to a healthier balance in the entire system of the universe, fostering diversity and peaceful coexistence.

The Ecology of Instinct: Sustainability through Instinctive Choices

We analyze the ecology of instinct, highlighting how our instinctive choices can influence the environment and the planet. Through examples of sustainable practices guided by instinct, we demonstrate how instinct can be a crucial ally in promoting responsible behaviors toward our habitat.

Chains of Consequence: How Individual Decisions Impact the Universe

We conclude the chapter by reflecting on the chains of consequence from individual and collective decisions. Providing examples of how instinct-based choices can create a cascading impact in the universe, we envision a world that is more harmonious and respectful of life in all its forms.

Through this chapter, readers will be guided to reconsider instinct not only as a personal force but as a bridge to a broader connection with the entire universal community. Respect for instinct not only contributes to individual fulfillment but extends as an act of responsibility and love toward global well-being and the balance of the universe.

Chapter 9: Living and Manifesting the Animal Instinct

The Animal Instinct: The Primordial Force Within Us

In this chapter, we delve into a deeper understanding of the "animal instinct." We explore how this primordial force, rooted in our being, can be a powerful guide in our daily lives. We analyze how the animal instinct represents intrinsic wisdom that connects us to our wild and authentic side.

Integration of Instinct: A Journey Toward Animal Awareness

We discuss the process of integrating instinct into our daily existence. We explore how we can embark on a journey toward greater animal awareness,

reconnecting with the primal
essence within us and embracing
the wisdom of the animal instinct.

**The Power of Presence: Living
in the Here and Now through
the Animal Instinct**

We delve into the concept of the
power of presence through the
animal instinct. We examine how
listening to this primordial force
allows us to live in the here and
now, breaking the chains of the
past and the future to embrace
the richness of the present
moment.

**Deciding Wisely: How the
Animal Instinct Guides Daily
Decisions**

We explore how the animal
instinct can wisely guide our daily
decisions. Through practical
advice, we illustrate how listening
to instinct in choices that shape
our destiny recognizes the animal

instinct as a reliable compass in the often turbulent waters of life.

Authentic Relationships: Cultivating Deep Connections through the Animal Instinct

We discuss the role of the animal instinct in cultivating authentic relationships. We explore how listening to this primordial force can enhance the quality of our interactions, allowing us to connect more deeply with others in an authentic and meaningful way.

Wild Creativity: Manifesting the Animal Instinct through Creative Expression

We analyze how the animal instinct can be manifested through creative expression. We explore how listening to this primordial force can unleash the wild creativity within each of us, enabling us to explore new artistic and innovative territories.

Practical Exercises: Integrating the Animal Instinct into Everyday Life

We provide a series of practical exercises to integrate the animal instinct into everyday life. From mindfulness practices to sensory exploration exercises, these practical tools will allow readers to tune into their animal nature and apply this awareness in every aspect of life.

The Cycle of Rebirth: Continuously Manifesting the Animal Instinct

We conclude the chapter with a reflection on the cycle of rebirth through the animal instinct. We emphasize how living and manifesting this primordial force is a continuous process of growth and renewal, a constant flow that connects us to the vitality of life itself.

Through this chapter, readers will be inspired to explore and embrace the animal instinct as a guiding force in their daily existence. Integrating this primordial wisdom will not only enrich their individual lives but also contribute to creating a world where the connection with our essential nature is honored and celebrated.

Chapter 10: The Ongoing Journey with Instinct

The Endless Voyage: Instinct as a Enduring Life Companion

In this final chapter, we explore the concept of the endless journey with instinct. We analyze how this vital connection can be a constant companion in our existence, guiding us through the various chapters of life with wisdom and intuition.

Continuous Adaptation: Maintaining the Connection with Instinct Amidst Changes

We discuss the importance of continuous adaptation in maintaining the connection with instinct. We examine how, faced with the inevitable changes of life, we can cultivate the mental flexibility needed to continue listening to instinct, even in new contexts and scenarios.

Guidance through Storms: Facing Challenges with Instinct at the Helm

We delve into how instinct can serve as a guide through the storms of life. We explore stories of individuals who, in the face of significant challenges, found in instinct a reliable compass, helping them navigate difficult waters and emerge stronger and wiser.

The Spirituality of Instinct: A Deep and Transcendental Path

We examine the concept of the spirituality of instinct, emphasizing how this connection can evolve into a deep and transcendental path. Through meditation and reflection practices, we explore how listening to instinct can lead us to a deeper understanding of our being and the meaning of life.

The Community of Instinct Listeners: Sharing Experiences and Growing Together

We discuss the formation of a community of individuals committed to listening to instinct. We explore how sharing experiences and learnings with others can enrich our journey, creating a network of support and mutual inspiration in exploring the depths of instinct.

The Beauty of Reflection: The Power of Continuous Introspection

We delve into the concept of the beauty of reflection in the ongoing listening to instinct. We examine how the practice of continuous introspection can strengthen the connection with instinct, offering us spaces to appreciate the beauty and depth of our inner experience.

The Innovation of Instinct: Embracing Constant Creativity in Living

We explore how instinct can be a constant engine of innovation in our lives. Through adopting a creative and open mindset, we show how we can continually reinvent our path, experimenting with new ways of listening and manifesting instinct.

Respect for Inevitable Change: Living with Acceptance and Gratitude

We conclude the chapter by reflecting on respect for inevitable change. We examine how, in the ongoing journey with instinct, we can learn to accept and embrace the flow of life with gratitude, recognizing that each phase brings valuable lessons and opportunities for growth.

Through this concluding chapter, we close the book by offering readers a forward-looking view of their journey with instinct. The ongoing journey is an invitation to explore, learn, and grow, keeping alive the connection with this primordial force that, when cultivated with awareness and respect, continues to guide us on an extraordinary journey through life.

Conclusion

In this journey through the pages of "Animal Wisdom: Practical Guide to Living and Manifesting Instinct," we have together explored the depths of our most authentic nature. We have delved into the intricacies of instinct, challenged the conventions of modern society, and learned to listen to that inner voice that knows wisdom without the need for explanations.

Each chapter has been a step toward a profound understanding of this primordial force that resides in each of us. But now, as we prepare to close this book, we want to extend an invitation to you: the invitation to action.

The true value of this guide lies in its practical application in your daily life. We challenge you to explore your daily decisions with the keen eye of instinct, to connect more deeply with others through animal wisdom, and to manifest your wild creativity in every moment.

The journey with instinct is a continuous commitment, a conscious choice to live with authenticity and awareness. We encourage you to put into practice the proposed exercises, to share your experiences with the community of instinct listeners, and to embrace every challenge as an opportunity for growth.

Remember that instinct is a faithful companion that can guide you through life's storms. Do not be afraid to listen to it, even when the path seems dark or uncertain. It is in listening to this inner voice that you will find the key to a more authentic, meaningful, and fulfilling life.

The future is uncharted territory, but you now have a reliable compass - your instinct. May the journey with instinct be your faithful companion, a beacon that lights the path of your existence. Move forward with courage, awareness, and gratitude, for every step is an opportunity to manifest your animal wisdom.

We wish you an extraordinary and passionate journey with instinct. May your life be permeated by awareness, enriched by wisdom, and illuminated by the light of your authenticity. Bon voyage!

www.ingramcontent.com/pod-product-compliance
Lightning Source LLC
Chambersburg PA
CBHW031308250726
48656CB00005B/1698